Steam Memories on Shed: 1950's – 1960's

No. 100: Scottish Region Eng
61A to 61C

David Dunn

Copyright Book Law Publications 2018
ISBN 978-1-909625-84-6

INTRODUCTION

With this album we look at the engine sheds provided mainly by the Great North of Scotland Railway and their constituents along with a major joint depot constructed in Aberdeen by the Caledonian and the North British railways. Tucked away in what was basically the north-east corner of the BR system, the 61A to 61C group of British Railways engine sheds was one of the smallest of the shed groups in terms of codes but within that list were a number of sub sheds catering for the numerous branch lines created to serve isolated communities.

Modellers have been catered for with some superb images of the obscure sub sheds, not to mention close-up views of locomotives of many classes, old and new. Hopefully some of you who have been contemplating starting a layout for some time will take the plunge with inspiration from this album.

Thanks to the Armstrong Railway Photographic Trust (ARPT) for the use of many of the images illustrated herein. Thanks also to those photographers who are acknowledged.

David Dunn, Cramlington, 2018.

(*Cover*)   **See page 29.**

(*Title page*)   **See page 7**

Printed and bound by The Amadeus Press, Cleckheaton, West Yorkshire
First published in the United Kingdom by Book Law Publications, 382 Carlton Hill, Nottingham, NG4 1JA

KITTYBREWSTER

D41 No.6819 on the Kittybrewster turntable in 1946. Still wearing its first LNER number and the wartime NE, the 4-4-0 became No.2231 on Sunday 29th September 1946 courtesy of a local painter at the shed. It got its BR number during a General overhaul at Inverurie in March 1948. It was condemned 21st November 1952, not quite the last of its class; the final three went during the following February which made Class D41 extinct. The Great North of Scotland Railway was probably unique amongst British railways in not having any 0-6-0 tender engines and instead it entrusted all of its trains, passenger and goods, to a fleet of one hundred 4-4-0 tender engines which were represented by fourteen classes. All of them became LNER property at Grouping but only two classes survived into BR ownership, D40 and D41, comprising twenty-one and twenty-nine engines respectively. With virtually half of the fleet being condemned prior to WW2, D31s from the North British section were brought in as replacements whilst B12s from the GE Area started to arrive from 1931. This image has actually been chosen to show the roofless portion of the roundhouse shed which was being transformed in 1946 to an open-fronted section; later BR did further alterations to the roof and frontage of the shed. The semi-roundhouse had an open turntable similar to the Highland Railway shed at Inverness; other examples are Guildford in Surrey, Horsham and Eastbourne in Sussex, St Blazey in Cornwall, and of course literally hundred in the United States. *K.H.Cockerill (ARPT).*

A splendid view of the area where two of the semi-roundhouses met; we are not sure of the dates when these two sheds were built but the different building styles are evident with stone arched entrances and a transverse pitched roof prevalent in the nearest section and simple square openings and transverse northlight roofs on the furthest section. However, that farthest section – containing seven stalls – had, up until the late 1930s, arched entrances on a stone frontage also but the roof is unchanged from the original pattern. A brick-built party wall existed between the two sheds giving further evidence of different dates; that particular wall is just discernible above the rainwater pipe. J72 No.68710 is shed pilot for the day (Wednesday 18th April 1951); it appears that light duties have been called because the 0-6-0T has just completed a General overhaul at Inverurie (the legend at the front corner of the running plate shows I 4-51. in true Inverurie style). The I equals Inverurie the rest is the month and year of repair. The LNER Group Standard tender has a DO NOT MOVE sign attached so perhaps the J72 is simply stabled awaiting some further business. *C.J.B.Sanderson (ARPT)*.

D41 No.62225 tucked away for the weekend on the siding alongside the footpath leading from the public road to the roundhouse. The date is 4th June 1950, a Sunday, and the shed is full, and quiet. The 4-4-0 was the class leader and was put into traffic in December 1893 along with five other members of the class turned out by Neilson & Co. as GNSR Class S, Nos.78 to 83. Between February 1895 and February 1898 another twenty-six similar Neilson-built engines – Class T – were put into traffic to form LNER Class D41 at Grouping. No.62225 was a Kittybrewster engine on this date but a transfer to Keith – its third stint there – took place during the final week of December 1950. That posting proved to be its last and on 20th February 1953, aged fifty-nine and a bit, the D41 was condemned. *C.J.B.Sanderson (ARPT)*.

The office of D41 No.62225 on that Sunday in June 1950; of note are the hidden two-handled metal shutters tucked away behind the sidesheets. The shutters would give a modicum of protection from the wind but these cabs remained a place where only the hardiest of folk trod, especially in winter, and going in reverse! *C.J.B.Sanderson (ARPT).*

When the B12s came to Kittybrewster from 1931 onwards they were the largest locomotives ever to work over the GNofSR metals. Strangely, they were welcomed by the Scottish enginemen and remained in top flight service until withdrawals started. This view of the yard on an unknown date in very early BR times, shows Nos.61524 (arrived Kittybrewster 24th April 1933) and 61529 (arrived Kittybrewster 10th July 1939) being serviced and made ready for their next jobs. Both engines are looking rather smart and this compiler suspects recent visits to main works maybe the reason. Inverurie shops had reverted back to applying LNER green to their charges shortly after the austere unlined black of WW2 livery was given up. Both of these engines had General overhauls in the summer of 1948, it was the last such event for No.61529 which was condemned on 3rd February 1950, so our date is looking more like that late summer of 1948 – note the flowers in bloom in the banking! Worthy of note is the two different types of boilers fitted. As further evidence of the date, is a new 16-ton mineral wagon – B49303 – on the old coaling bank to the left; that wagon was constructed by Hurst Nelson & Co. at about the year in question; 16-ton mineral wagons did not last too long in service looking like that. Of course neither engine has acquired a front numberplate or any BR insignia of any kind although lining is in place. No.61524 transferred to Keith on 7th July 1953 but was condemned four months later on Bonfire Night whilst attending works at Inverurie. Behind the 4-6-0s stands the huge coaling plant so thoughtfully provided by the LNER and supplied by Henry Lees & Co. in 1932; the appliance was reportedly the most northerly concrete coaling plant on British Railways. *A.R. Thompson coll. (ARPT).*

B12 No.61513 beneath the Kittybrewster coaling plant in 1949; a front numberplate is now in place, and BRITISH RAILWAYS adorns the tender sides. No.61513 was a latecomer to service in Scotland having arrived at Kittybrewster in June 1940, straight after a General overhaul at Stratford. *K.H.Cockerill (ARPT).*

Tucked away at the back of the shed site at the southern end, alongside the public entrance '...a cinder path leads to...' in October 1953 was a newly arrived D34 from Eastfield. No.62480 GLEN FRUIN still had the 65A shed plate attached and the Eastfield legend on the bufferbeam. The 4-4-0 is in steam and has probably just arrived from Glasgow. It is situated out of sight, hidden even. As though Kittybrewster staff have spirited it away for the time being! It may well have been the 13th of the month, the official transfer date? It is yet another former North British Railway locomotive to add to the growing band of residents at 61A. Of further interest is the shed behind the tender. Was this the original 4-road engine shed superseded by the semi-roundhouse? Alas, the Kittybrewster complex is long gone so we may never know! *J.D.Mills, M.Halbert collection.*

The GNofSR possessed just four tank locomotives and these only because of a requirement by the Aberdeen Harbour Commissioners to have locomotives fitting into their stipulated weight restrictions for working onto the docks. The first two were delivered from makers Manning Wardle & Co., in January 1915, were actually two-tons over the limit and these later became LNER Class Z5. In August 1915 Manning Wardle delivered two more 0-4-2T which weighed some five tons less than the January engines and were therefore well below the AHC limit. These engines became LNER Class Z4 and were similar in every way to their larger sisters but were simply scaled down. This 15th April 1949 image shows off nicely the subtle difference and the not so subtle differences between the Z5 No.68193 and Z4 No.68190. Eventually the AHC raised their weight limit which enabled the two heavier engines to undertake dock working whenever required. The other pair of the four were Z4 No.68191 and Z5 No.68192. Note that both of these engines had the BRITISH RAILWAYS livery with full BR numbers at this time. Of course having four such locomotives where two were originally planned meant a surplus so all four locomotives spent long periods in store especially during BR days. *A.R. Thompson collection. (ARPT).*

63E Oban based Drummond 1883 2F No.57254 hangs around the servicing area in Kittybrewster shed yard on Wednesday 18th April 1951 as though it doesn't want to return to the west coast. Ex-works – another image showing the right front side of the engine reveals the Inverurie works date of 2-51 – the 0-6-0 has a specially adapted tender protecting the coal space (and the crew) when working a large independent snowplough tender first. No.57254 transferred to Ardrossan in August 1955 but it is not known if that special tender went with it. Kittybrewster took in all the ex-works locomotives from Inverurie and after running them in would use them for certain jobs in place of one of their own. Note the placing of the shed plate above the running number. *C.J.B.Sanderson (ARPT)*.

B12 No.61524 again but in the summer of 1952 after its last Heavy Intermediate overhaul; now in fully lined black, the 4-6-0 is in its final livery before withdrawal. Making its way from the servicing area, No.61524 will move onto the turntable and then be given a stall in the semi-roundhouse. This view reveals some of the shed roof which at this time had pitches topped off with smoke vents. The door on the left had seen better days but engine shed doors were not known for their longevity especially at busy depots. *C.J.B.Sanderson (ARPT)*.

(*opposite, top*) Two same day photographs of ex-Inverurie works locomotives at Kittybrewster shed on 30th August 1952. J36 No.65247 was in fact a resident of 61A and had been 'off works' since the previous 1st March. Its external appearance is something of a mystery but note that it has yet to receive the small version of the BR emblem on its tender side, not to mention the power classification and route availability information on the cab sides. (*opposite, bottom*) Grangemouth based 2F No.57366 looking quite splendid after a spell in works. It seems that Inverurie had ceased to paint the works date on the front corner of the running plate at this date. *Both C.J.B.Sanderson (ARPT)*.

An early morning view of one of Thompson's B1 4-6-0s beneath the Kittybrewster coaler. Kittybrewster received twenty-eight examples of this numerous and successful class between August 1946 and May 1950. They came from all the workshops and contractors involved in their construction and the annual rate of delivery was as follows: 1946 – 2; 1947 – 7; 1948 – 5; 1949 – 9; 1950 – 5. They were, it will be noted, replacing the B12s. No.61350 shown on 30th August 1952 was delivered from Darlington on 28th July 1949. Like many of the B1s still allocated to 61A in June 1961, No.61350 moved on but only across the city to Ferryhill. It ended its days at Dunfermline shed in November 1966. *C.J.B.Sanderson (ARPT).*

When Kittybrewster got its first BR Standard Cl.4 tank engines in October and November 1951 – Nos.80020 and 80021 – direct from Brighton, they must have thought they were early Christmas presents. When the next new pair turned up during the following January – Nos.80028 and 80029 also from Brighton – they knew they had. Exactly a year after the pioneer pair had arrived, another pair came in November 1952 – Nos.80004 and 80005 direct from Derby – so they knew that Christmas had come early once again. Just when things had settled down and the 2-6-4T were all running nicely on Kittybrewster duties all over NE Scotland, another batch of new locomotives were sent to 61A from Doncaster – Nos.80106 to 80110 – during October and November 1954. The summer of 1955 brought two more Brighton-built engines to 61A – 80121 and 80122 – but only briefly because in November they transferred to Keith a move which basically kept them 'in the fold.' During May and June 1957 five more of the class were sent from Polmadie to Kittybrewster, second-hand this time – Nos.80111 to 80115 – but still in fairly fine fettle (considering the high mileage's) and in numerical sequence to the last lot received. However, that Doncaster batch numbered 80106 to 80110 were actually transferred away to Polmadie, swapped for the high mileage engines. If Kittybrewster had kept that five instead of having to swap, they would have had all of the Doncaster Cl.4 tank production under one roof. Alas such niceties were not necessarily part of BR's philosophy. Three of the latter batch went to Keith in 1960 whereas the rest left 61A in June 1961 as dieselisation took hold. The reign of the BR Cl.4 tanks at Kittybrewster was brief but it was nice. This is No.80021 – complete with miniature snowplough – being serviced in April 1953. Note the covered recess in the lower section of the cab side sheet; that was for the Manson tablet exchange gear. *C.J.B.Sanderson (ARPT).*

15

Something the GNofSR never really invested in was tank locomotives (although one venture in 1915 cost them dearly) so it was no surprise that the LNER and later BR would shower Kittybrewster shed with tank engines of various sizes. The former NER J72 was a good all round performer and Kittybrewster had a number of them allocated over the years. This is No.68719 in April 1953 stood near the coaling plant; leaving NE Area in March 1932, the six-coupled tank never returned south – it probably never ventured south of Aberdeen – even its shopping was carried out at Inverurie, as was its demise a week after being condemned on 24th January 1961. *C.J.B.Sanderson (ARPT).*

With further glimpses of the shed's architecture to be gleamed, we watch BR Std. Cl.4 No.80028 using the Kittybrewster turntable on 30th August 1952. The Brighton works plate must have seemed a strange appendage to any local who was ignorant to the facts of this locomotive's origins. After the Standards' left Kittybrewster in 1961 their fortunes waxed and waned along with all the other steam locomotives of that period. The diesel reigned – but not supremely – but many of the 61A enginemen must have wished for these 2-6-4Ts to return if only for some reliability. *C.J.B.Sanderson (ARPT)*.

By now a long-standing member of the Kittybrewster stud, ex-LMS 2P No.40650, with full lining and the new BR crest, is stabled in 61A's yard on Monday 22nd August 1960. Four of the shed's former LMS 2Ps survived the closure to steam motive power and they all transferred – on paper at least – to Ferryhill depot from where they were withdrawn in October 1961. Whether they actually went to 61B is unknown but they all made the short trip to Inverurie for cutting up. Their numbers: 40618, 40648, 40650, and 40663. Interloper Andrew Barclay D24xx shunts cattle wagons in the distance. *C.J.B.Sanderson (ARPT).*

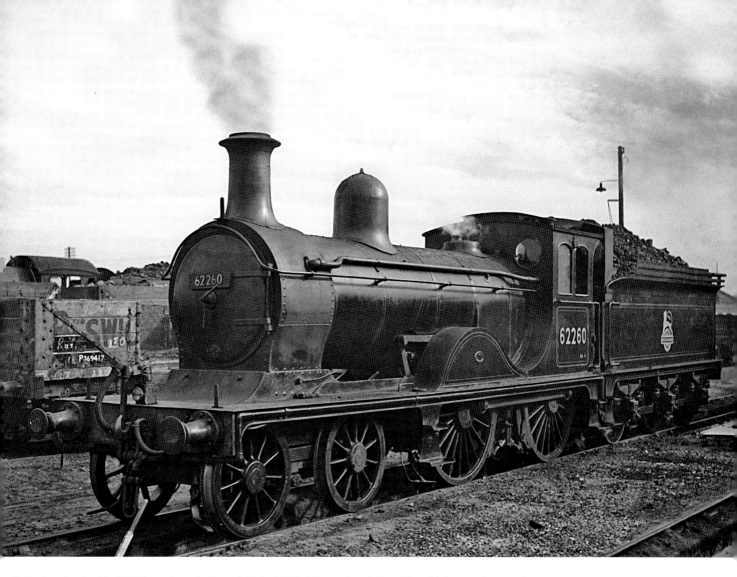

D40 class leader No.62260 on the ash pits at 61A in 1952 with a rather full tender which was also sporting one of the detachable cab plates which gave greater protection when working tender first especially but was also useful in keeping some of the weather off when running chimney first. The rather large 28in. high BR lion-and-wheel emblem was put on during a General overhaul in November 1949 and was the first emblem carried by a D40. The transfer looked too big for that tender and this example proved to be the only one applied. This locomotive had five different numbers during its lifetime: No.116 on delivery in August 1899; No.25 from 31st January 1900; No.6825 from 1st April 1924; No.2260 from 2nd October 1946; and finally No.62260 from 18th December 1948. *C.J.B.Sanderson (ARPT).*

Resident No.62276 ANDREW BAIN alongside the roundhouse on 30th August 1952. The D41 looks rather smart and considering it was more than six months since its last works visit, the shed staff had certainly looked after their charge. No.62276 spent its entire life at Kittybrewster from its arrival in October 1920 from makers North British Locomotive Co. to its demise on 25th August 1955. It was taken to Kilmarnock for breaking up during the following November, and en route it passed its place of birth. This image allows us to see the seven pitches which made up the roof over this area of the roundhouse; each pitch note has its own smoke ventilator. *C.J.B.Sanderson (ARPT).*

By the end of BR's first full decade, Kittybrewster shed had a sizeable D34 stud including this rather down-at-heel example stabled near the coaler on Wednesday 26th August 1959. No.62489 GLEN DESSARY had not been near works for seventeen months and it was beginning to show because by 1959 most of the engine sheds around the United Kingdom were starting to find difficulty in recruiting staff for the footplate grades where beginners started with a pile of rags and a bucket of paraffin, for locomotive cleaning purposes. Kittybrewster was no exception and its allocation was suffering too. However, help was at hand and on 18th December 1959 our subject here was condemned. By the end of the following March it was taken into Inverurie and cut up. End of problem, or was it? The D34s were drafted into 61A to help fill the gaps left by both the decreasing fleet of ex-GNofSR 4-4-0s and the B12s which were starting to disappear into scrapyards. For the record, the following D34s transferred from the Central Belt sheds to 61A during BR times as follows: Nos.62469 GLEN DOUGLAS – 29th March 1953; 62479 GLEN SHEIL – 15th February 1953; 62480 GLEN FRUIN – 7th October 1953; 62482 GLEN MAMIE – 7th October 1953; 62489 GLEN DESSARY – 25th January 1953; 62493 GLEN GLOY – 25th January 1953; 62497 GLEN MALLIE – 17th May 1953; 62498 GLEN MOIDART – 10th May 1954. They all ended their days on the former GNofSR lines except No.62469. Then there was an earlier generation of ex-NBR locomotives from Class D31 which worked from Kittybrewster in LNER days thus: No.9575; 9634; 9642 (62282); 9037; 9404 (2062); 9211; 9212; 9215; 9216; 9729; 9730; 9731; 9732 (62065); 9733 (2066); 9734 (2067); 9735; 9736; 9737; 9738; 9739 (2068); 9740 (2069); 9765; 9767 (2071); 9768 (62072); 9769 (2073); 9770 (2074). Finally, note the wrong facing BR crest adorning the tender. Now there was something which would never be put right, or was that left? *Howard Forster.*

GORDON HIGHLANDER straddling the turntable on that same Saturday in August 1952. No.62277 was another Keith based engine which was coaled, watered, and now turned ready to work home. Note that the shortage of small sized BR emblems has forced the 4-4-0 to be put into traffic with no corporate identity. Considering that the D41 had attended works back in June for a Heavy overhaul, you would have thought that such things as emblem transfers would have been available by now but such was the period in British history when many everyday items were still under ration or altogether shortages. Nowadays, you've never had it so good! This view of the roundhouse reveals

ten smoke vents atop the pitched roof of what was the last section of the shed to be altered. *C.J.B.Sanderson (ARPT).*

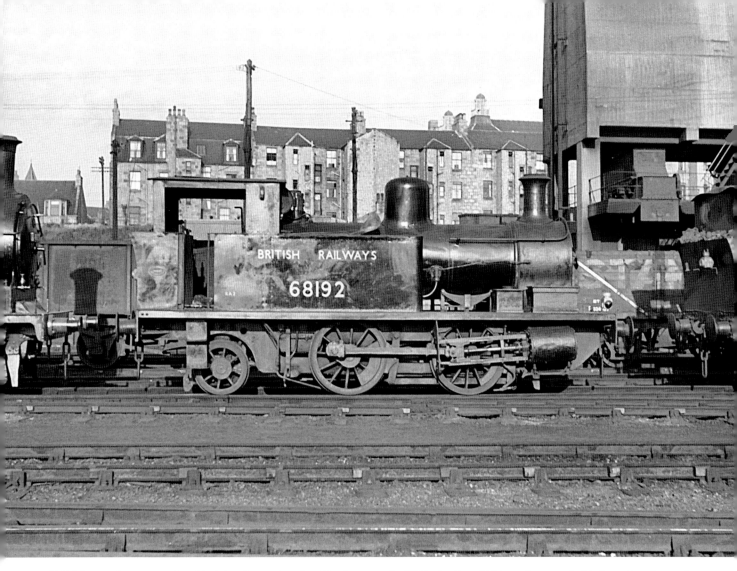

Z5 No.68192 in employment and stabled for the weekend at Kittybrewster in 1950; the four 'Zs' lasted a remarkably long time in service considering their employment record was somewhat chequered. All but No.68193 went through the full gambit of liveries on offer up to 1957; the odd-man-out was withdrawn on 24th April 1956 and so took the BR lettering livery with it to the scrapyard at Inverurie. The other went as follows: No.68191 on 31st March 1959, Nos.68190 and 68192 both on 28th April 1960. *K.H.Cockerill (ARPT)*.

One of the two Kittybrewster snow ploughs as at 23rd June 1957. The appliance looks to be fashioned from an old brake van but may well have been specially built from the outset considering its importance – the other unit was an exact twin. The legend on the side states: N.E. LOCO DEPT, 981511, SNOWPLOUGH, KITTYBREWSTER. The business end looks like an old Dreadnought battleship prow. When it was actually constructed is unknown but it must have done what was asked of it for decades because people in this part of the world do not waste money. Obviously it was strategically weighed but one can't help but wonder how many times it was derailed during snow clearing operations. *C.J.B.Sanderson (ARPT).*

All shapes and sizes of former Caledonian Railway locomotives visited Inverurie for shopping and afterwards attended Kittybrewster for running-in. This is 63C Forfar based 2P 0-4-4T No.55198 on 23rd June 1957 fully coaled and waiting for action near to the depot's pedestrian entrance; note the aforementioned cinder path. It will be also noted by the eagle-eyed readers that Inverurie had restored their shopping date legend to the front end of the running plate bracket and this example shows I 6-57. Both Inverurie and Kittybrewster became the 'must visit' venues for spotters' nation-wide, the variety and rarity of some of their occupants made the whole long journeys worth it. *C.J.B.Sanderson (ARPT)*.

Last word on Kittybrewster: April 1953; with a full tender of coal, newly arrived resident D34 No.62479 GLEN SHEIL stands on Breakdown train duty. It will be noted that it is heading north to cover the former GNofSR lines. The lines to the south of Aberdeen would require another engine facing south for running purposes, assuming one was available; if not our subject might have to run tender first! This former Eastfield engine transferred to 61A in February 1953 and remained to withdrawal in June 1961. All of its shopping was carried out at Inverurie after its arrival from Glasgow; it was even broken up there in 1961. *C.J.B.Sanderson (ARPT).*

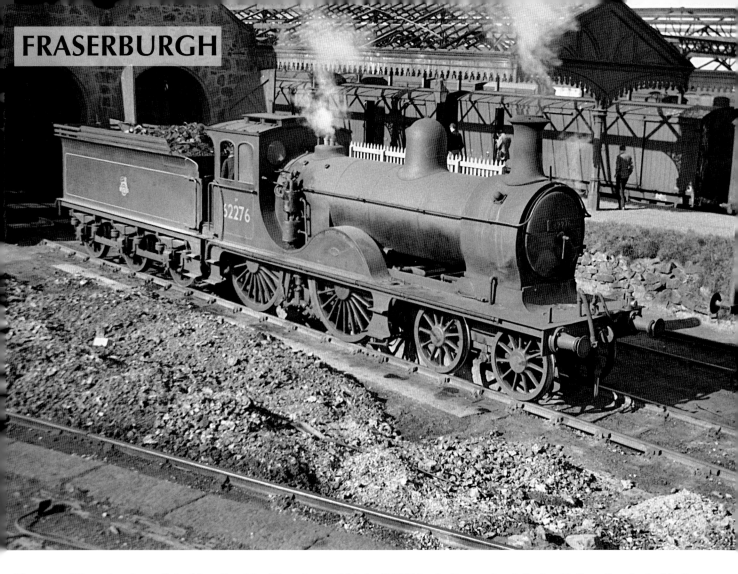

The town of Fraserburgh was linked by rail to Maud Junction on 24th April 1965 by the Formartine & Buchan Railway Co. who had built a 15-mile line from the junction with the Peterhead line. In July 1866 the whole line became GNofSR property. The engine shed opened at the same time as the railway and was built in the contemporary style with stone walls enclosing two dead-ended roads. This image recorded on 28th May 1955 shows one of the superheated D40s, No.62276 ANDREW BAIN, bathing in the afternoon sun awaiting its next duty. Kittybrewster supplied all the motive power for this sub shed which at this time could have done with some manual labour to clear the accumulating ash piles. This 4-4-0 was just three months away from withdrawal and replacements were arriving from the south-west of Scotland in the shape of LMS-built 2P 4-4-0s which in this compiler's eyes were about the least attractive of all the 4-4-0s which ever worked in the UK! The adjacent station, shown with various vans for the fish traffic, was operating until 4th October 1965 whereas the engine shed succumbed in June 1961 with the cessation of steam services. Goods services survived until 1979. Even when the railway existed, Fraserburgh, along with Peterhead, were recognised as the most distant towns in the United Kingdom from anywhere else of similar size. *F.W.Hampson (ARPT).*

Wearing one of the painted versions of nameplate, D40 No.62274 BENACHIE is another afternoon capture but on an unknown date. To give us a chance of pinning down a date, we know that this 4-4-0 was transferred from Keith to 61A on 7th July 1954, it was condemned on 20th September 1955 so we are somewhere between those dates. Note that the ash piles were growing so perhaps we are some weeks after No.62276's sojourn in May 1955? *A.R. Thompson collection. (ARPT).*

Ivatt Cl.2 No.46460 comes off the turntable road at Fraserburgh ready for another working to St Combs. It will be noted that the 2MT was equipped with the so-called cow-catcher apparatus for working the branch from Fraserburgh to St Combs which was unfenced for much of its length and which ran over open farmland with livestock roaming un-tethered! It is unknown if the catcher was a bespoke fabrication for the 2-6-0 or if it had been taken off another older locomotive which had passed on to pastures anew – a number of former Great Eastern F4 tank locomotives (67151, 67157, 67164) worked from Fraserburgh shed during LNER days and the early BR period, and a couple of these were fitted with brackets to carry the cow catchers; they also had sliding shutters or windows fitted to their cabs to protect crews from the bitter easterly winds experienced on the branch. A catcher was fitted to both ends of No.46460 thereby negating the requirement for a turntable at the St Combs end of the branch; the cab afforded enough protection without the need to add further windows or shutters. No.46460 was transferred to Kittybrewster from St Margarets in January 1952 and remained the only member of that class to be allocated to 61A for any length of time – it moved on to Keith in May 1960. Whenever it was away at works another Ivatt Cl.2 was transferred in on a temporary basis to cover for its absence; sisters Nos.46461 and 46464 both stood in at various times as did some of the other Scottish region based engines. *C.J.B.Sanderson (ARPT).*

The 'engine shed' at Inverurie locomotive works consisted this stabling point complete with its own engine pit – no shed ever existed. This particular site is the second such area given over to stabling the works pilot engines; an earlier site, just west of this point and established in 1901, was required for the expansion of the erecting shops prior to Grouping. Motive power for the works pilot (A 18) was supplied by Kittybrewster and on 23rd June 1957 J72 No.68710 was doing the honours. The 0-6-0T arrived at Kittybrewster from Keith on 5th April 1932, one of a number of J72s transferred from North Eastern Area during that time. It remained at 61A until withdrawn on 5th March 1959; it was sold for scrap in August to a yard in Wishaw; this event coincided with the employment of a diesel shunter as works pilot from thereon. In the background St Margarets based N15 No.69186 has just completed a Light Intermediate (4th–21st June) and is looking very smart in its newly applied lined black livery. The 0-6-2T was condemned 31st July 1959 and then cut up at Inverurie in October. *C.J.B.Sanderson (ARPT).*

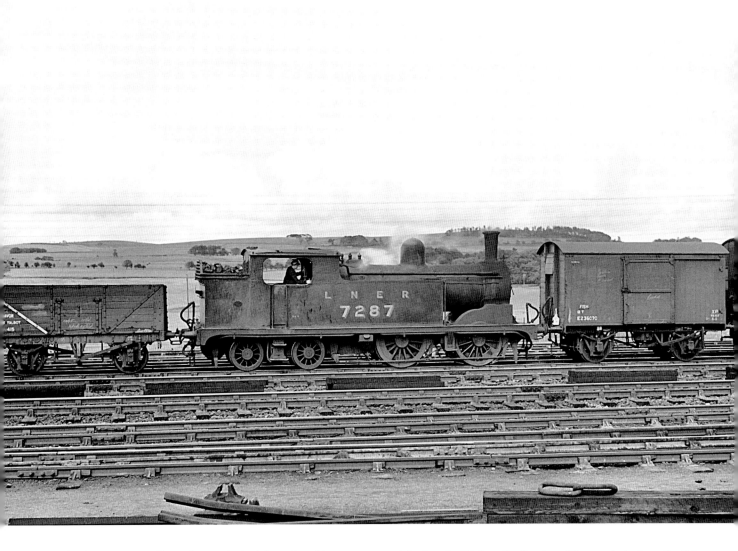

G5 No.(6)7287 was works pilot at Inverurie in this undated image captured during the Nationalisation transition period when the 0-4-4T carried its last LNER number (applied 25th May 1946 during a 'Light' at Inverurie). Its BR number was put on in June 1950 at Kittybrewster shed. This engine was another orphan from the North East Area but arrived during WW2 in July 1940 from South Blyth. Its last stint at Inverurie started 24th March 1947 and ended when it was condemned on 31st March 1953. Note the coal hopper with its cut-away side cage; although a standard fitting in NE Area, other shed areas regarded the cages as a nuisance and cut the sides off to allow better access to the bunker when coaling the engines at the manual stages. Pushing and pulling stock during shunting operations, the G5 has an interesting 10-ton open in tow; it is marked Glenavon, Port Talbot No.415! *A.R. Thompson (ARPT)*.

MACDUFF

Later in this album a similar image to this one is illustrated showing the engine shed at Banff which was not too far from Macduff, as-the-crow-flies, was on the same coast, indeed the same estuary, and in a location which was also overlooked by high ground; not to mention both locations were in sight of each other. Images such as this give the reader a sense of knowing the place straight away. It gives modellers who have yet to finalise a layout idea a reason to start now on something just like this. So, having got the tasty treats handed out let us look at Macduff terminus with its single island platform half hidden by a substantial overall roof. Our engine shed is tucked away in this bottom left corner whilst the passenger and goods stations are generously afforded land on the available open ground. The signal box overlooks everything, just like a control centre should. The date is 20th April 1951, a Friday, with very little happening except for a pair of platelayers with a trolley seeing to a points problem in the goods yard. Across the main road three motor vehicles are attending the Esso garage whilst a fourth heads east towards the harbour. The changes in elevation are quite apparent here with the railway holding the intermediate ground above the shore line properties. The shed yard contains a turntable at the eastern end along with the stone base water tank. *C.J.B.Sanderson (ARPT).*

An undated photograph of Kittybrewster based D40 No.62277 GORDON HIGHLANDER standing outside the soon to be closed engine shed. The shed was built by the GNofSR in 1872, the second such establishment on the branch because it superseded a Banff, Macduff & Turriff Junction Railway shed built in 1860 at Banff Bridge when the branch was extended to the seaside location. This shed here closed on 1st October 1951 so the presence of the 4-4-0 must have been towards the end although No.62277 was turned out from Inverurie in this condition – fully lined – on 13th November 1948. The timber post topped off with a gas light has recently received a coat of paint so something was afoot. Macduff station closed with the line also on 1st October 1951; eight intermediate stations on the branch also got the chop! *A.R. Thompson collection. (ARPT).*

The closed and abandoned Macduff engine shed at some time during the 1950s. Never a busy line, the first timetables showed just three return passenger trains and one freight train a day; this was soon changed to three mixed trains. After closure to passenger services, the branch remained open for goods traffic until 1966 and no doubt a daily pick-up goods would service all the necessary facilities on the line. The dead-ended, stone-built shed was apparently untouched by change throughout its lifetime and may even have retained the original as opened bespoke doors. It was reported that the building was still in use during the 1990s as a store for fishing nets but its status now is unknown. Yes, that is Banff across the water also known as the River Deveron. Why a railway bridge was never constructed to carry the lines across to link Banff with Macduff is unknown because road traffic was catered for from an early age. *A.R. Thompson collection. (ARPT).*

PETERHEAD

Peterhead engine shed consisted a two-road, dead-ended stone built structure with a slated roof. The shed was opened in July 1862 by the Formartine & Buchan Railway Co. and later absorbed (July 1866) by the GNofSR. The building survived until closed on 3rd May 1965; the shed had actually closed to steam in June 1961 in line with others in that area of the region. Demolition followed soon afterwards. The passenger station had closed on the same day but goods services continued until 1970. The shed can be seen behind D40 No.62278 HATTON CASTLE which is stabled alongside a coaling wagon on 17th October 1952. The Kittybrewster based 2P it will be noted no longer has the Westinghouse brake connection, the pumps being removed and replaced by steam brakes and vacuum ejector in July 1940. The other hose at this end of the locomotive is a heating connection fitted in June 1947. K.BREWSTER and D40 are discernible on the bufferbeam in the Inverurie style. *R.K. Taylor (ARPT).*

(*above and below*) A rather smart looking No.62265 outside Peterhead shed on Friday 20th April 1951 just five weeks after the D40 had completed a 'General' at Inverurie (17th February to 10th March). No.62265 transferred to Keith on 16th September 1951 and very likely never came this was again. *Both C.J.B.Sanderson (ARPT).*

Not so clean 2P No.40603 runs alongside the turntable at Peterhead during the evening on 28th May 1955. Another Kittybrewster steed, these ex-LMS 4-4-0s never had the same appeal to the former Great North enginemen and so would more than likely accumulate dirt somewhat quicker than the 'local' engines they were brought in to replace. *F.W.Hampson (ARPT)*.

ABERDEEN FERRYHILL

N15 No.69201 is totally at home in Aberdeen's Ferryhill engine shed on 28th May 1955. The former North British 0-6-2T (NB design but LNER built; to traffic 1st March 1923) had actually been allocated to Dunfermline for all of its life up to 18th December 1949 when it transferred to Aberdeen to join sisters Nos.69128 and 69129. Being a joint shed when opened in 1908, both Caledonian Railway and North British Railway locomotives could be found allocated here albeit in their respective sections of the building. The coaling and turning facilities were shared and even then both companies were mature enough to accept each other's requirements after decades of venomous rhetoric from both parties. Behind the N15 is the single road manual coaling stage which had gone through numerous cladding changes over the previous forty-odd years, its latest covering being corrugated materials which have been partly renewed. Returning to our tank locomotive, No.69201 was transferred to Keith on 16th December 1957 but three weeks later it was condemned and then sent to Kilmarnock for scrapping during the following March. Which begs the question – did it ever move to Keith? *F.W.Hampson (ARPT)*.

An undated view of Dundee based V2 No.60836 calling at the coaling stage for a top-up prior to turning and being made ready to work home. The V2 transferred to Dundee quite late in the day on 13th April 1964 so this image is post April 64' we can assume. Prior to its stint at 62B, No.60836 was allocated here at Ferryhill for five months along with No.60835. Already the V2 has been given the Dundee treatment with silvered (painted) door hinges, handles, shed plates, and V-2 along with DUNDEE painted on the bufferbeam! The works at Darlington spent two months giving this locomotive a Casual Light overhaul shortly after Dundee acquired it, and that shopping appears to have given the V2 a second wind because it was not condemned until the last day of 1966. *D.R. Dunn collection. (ARPT).*

As viewed from an inspection pit in the repair shop, A4 No.60007 SIR NIGEL GRESLEY arrives at Ferryhill shed in 1964. Although the Pacific didn't visit any main works south of the border after the summer of 1963, it did make three appearances at Inverurie for Non-Classified repairs in 1964 and 1965 whilst allocated at 61B. *I.W.Coulson (ARPT).*   43

We don't have an exact date for this image, just 1963! On 25th November 1963 J38 No.65900 was condemned. Where that event took place is unknown; was it at its home shed Thornton Junction or here at Ferryhill after a defect was found during a routine working to Aberdeen? It may well have been en route to Inverurie for overhaul and main works withdrew the 0-6-0? The fact that the coupling rods are removed and the tender appears to be empty would bolster that latter theory. Whatever the circumstances behind the image, No.65900 was cut up at Inverurie in 1963, one of only two of her class scrapped there. *IW.Coulson (ARPT).*

44

F4 No.67157 with its cow-catchers fore and aft for working the St Combs branch – note the sliding cab shutters too. Now what was it doing at Ferryhill on 13th September 1955? Note the long redundant destination board brackets on the smokebox door! The F4 had come north to Aberdeen in January 1948 from Yarmouth Beach. The cowcatchers were fitted at Inverurie in February 1948. Perhaps by now the 2-4-2T was a lost soul by now with the Ivatt Cl.2 running the branch services from Fraserburgh; during the following June aged 49 years and 1 month, No.67157 was condemned and then cut up at Inverurie. Transferred from Polmadie in September 1954, Stanier Cl.5 No.45162 stables alongside the F4. *C.J.B.Sanderson (ARPT).*

A3s were becoming 'thin on the ground' at Ferryhill by 1963 so it was always nice to see visitors working into the city and then coming on shed. One such visitor was No.60094 COLORADO from St Rollox which was also involved with the 3-hour expresses; the A3 had moved from Eastfield to 65B on 14th January 1963 and remained at St Rollox until withdrawn in February 1964. Ferryhill's very own resident A3 No.60042 SINGAPORE, similarly fitted with German-type smoke deflectors, can be seen through the opening on the left – 60042 transferred to 61B on 7th April 1963 ex Heaton; it left for St Margarets on 27th October 1963. From the dates given above we can round up the date to anywhere between April and October. *IW.Coulson (ARPT).*

Peppercorn A2 No.60531 BARHAM graces Ferryhill shed yard on 18th April 1951. Starting life at Gateshead shed on 12th March 1948, the A2 joined 61B's stud on 7th August 1949 remaining until transferred to York on 2nd December 1962. However, that particular transfer was never enacted because No.60531 had been inside Doncaster 'Plant' works since 29th October 1962 awaiting a new boiler; it was in fact never overhauled and was instead condemned on 10th December 1962. Ferryhill had a number of these superb locomotives allocated: No.60525 A.H.PEPPERCORN – 28th August 1949 (ex-New England) to 27th March 1963 (Condemned); 60527 SUN CHARIOT – 28th May 1960 (ex-Perth) to 15th September 1963 (to Polmadie); 60528 TUDOR MINSTREL – 28th May 1960 (ex-Perth) to 19th June 1961 (to Dundee) and 24th April 1966 (ex-Dundee) to 2nd June 1966 (Condemned); 60532 BLUE PETER – see later; 60537 BACHELORS BUTTON – 1st July 1949 (ex-New England) to 7th January 1951 (to Haymarket). *C.J.B.Sanderson (ARPT).*

C16 No.67496 was one of only two C16s allocated to Ferryhill – No.67501 was the other – and both engines arrived in Aberdeen during 1951, No.67501 in September and 67496 in November. This image illustrates 67496 on the shed yard on 3rd March 1953 shortly after 67496's arrival back from a Casual Light repair at Cowlairs when the legend FERRYHILL was applied to the bufferbeam amongst other things. However, on 16th March the Atlantic tank was taken into Inverurie – for the first and last time – for a Non-Classified repair; it returned to 61B on the 19th March. The 4-4-2Ts were employed on the Stonehaven locals, one of the few suburban jobs entrusted to Ferryhill shed. On 8th October 1956 No.67496 was transferred to Keith followed by sister 67501 in April 1957 – the DMUs had arrived! St Margarets based J36 No.65327 stables alongside and is turned awaiting a working home, a tidy journey indeed but one probably broken up with a stop at Dundee Tay Bridge shed. *F.W.Hampson (ARPT)*.

Perth based 'Jubilee' No.45575 MADRAS coaled, turned and ready to work home on 4th June 1950. This North British-built 4-6-0 had initially been allocated to four English sheds but in 1936 it was sent north to Corkerhill remaining in Scotland until the end of August 1952 when it became one of the fleet of low-mileage Scottish Region engines swapped for a similar number of higher mileage Jubilees working from English depots. Its transfer to Perth was only a few months old when this image was recorded having moved from Corkerhill on 1st April 1950. No.45575 carries one of the original dome-less boilers – No.8750 – which remained so having never been converted to domed type (Nos.8748 to 8752 were the examples which hung on to the end and were scrapped with the respective engines carrying them). Note the St Rollox placing of the cab side power classification code 6P beneath the running number a practice used at English works during LMS days but after Nationalisation the classification was placed above the number. Although many of the ex-LMS 'hierarchy' used to work into Aberdeen on trains from Perth and Glasgow, including the Pacifics, only five 'Jubilees' – Nos.45579, 45580, 45643, 45644 (October 1935 to March 1939), and 45729 (May to November 1937) – were ever allocated to Ferryhill and all of them afterwards went to Kingmoor. Of course two original 'Royal Scots' were also resident, Nos.6121 from September 1935 to June 1936, and 6138 from April 1935 to June 1937. The LNER it seems had entrusted more of their front-line express passenger locomotives over the decades since 1923 to the care of Ferryhill; not to mention two of the six the eight-coupled P2s. *C.J.B.Sanderson (ARPT).* 49

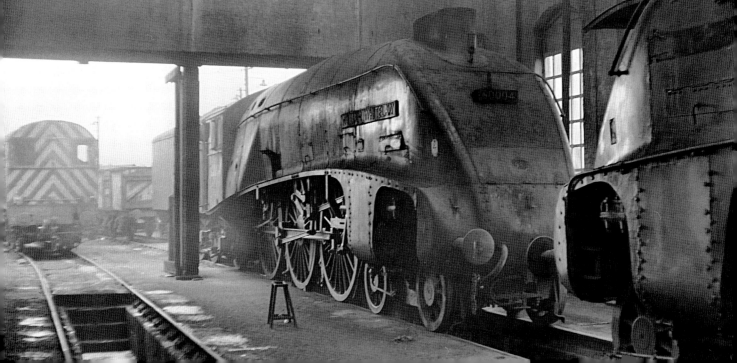

(*opposite, top*) There is a reason why these two A4s – Nos.60009 and 60004 – were residing in the repair shop at Ferryhill in July 1966. Tenderless UNION OF SOUTH AFRICA, also minus nameplates, had just given up its corridor tender (No.5332) after being withdrawn on 1st June. That tender had been sold by BR to Alan Pegler for use behind FLYING SCOTSMAN but No.60009's new owners also wanted an 8-wheel corridor tender coupled to their new purchase. By 1966 A4 tenders, especially the corridor type, were becoming fairly rare but luckily for BR, and 60009, one of Ferryhill's A4s, No.60004 WILLIAM WHITELAW was coupled to the unique No.5484, the 5000-gallon, 8-wheel, corridor tender built at Doncaster in 1929 especially for the 'Hush-Hush' No.10000 (60700). The parties concerned were all happy with the outcome and No.60004 duly gave up its tender to No.60009 in that July 1966 swap. (*opposite, bottom*) Opened mouthed, No.60009 awaits events whilst No.60004 is just condemned – 17th July – ready for sale to a yard in Wishaw, minus that all important tender of course. No.5484 would require turning but that diesel shunter and the 70-foot turntable would sort that out – was that the first time a 350 h.p. diesel shunter had used the turntable? It would be interesting to know which tender did accompany No.60004 on its journey south. *D.R. Dunn collection. (ARPT).*

(*right*) **Peppercorn A2 No.60532 BLUE PETER spent most of its BR operational life allocated to Aberdeen's Ferryhill depot. Transferred to 61B on 7th January 1951 from Haymarket, the Pacific worked from the shed until moved to Dundee on 19th June 1961. On 4th December 1966 No.60532 was officially returned to Ferryhill's books but only until the end of the year when withdrawal took place. This image is undated except for the note 1966 so it could have been taken at any time during that year as the A2 was a regular visitor to Aberdeen.** *D.R. Dunn collection. (ARPT).*

The two Gresley V4s – BR Nos.61700 and 61701 – spent most of their lives working at various sheds in Scotland (No.61700 as No.3401 did a trial stint of eight months on the Great Eastern section during the early years of WW2) and on 24th May 1954 both of them were transferred from Eastfield to Ferryhill. Whilst at 61B they worked passenger services to Perth besides good trains to Dundee. In February 1957 No.61701 is seen on the shed yard at Ferryhill during the pair's final months of operation. No.61700 was already at Cowlairs on this date and it was decided not to repair her; she was sent to Kilmarnock during the following May and cut up. Our subject here did not fare much better and although No.61701 remained operational until the end of November, she too was sent for breaking up at the works in Kilmarnock during February 1958. *C.J.B.Sanderson (ARPT).*

The end is nigh! This is V2 No.60888, one of the V4s older and larger sisters, which was in dire straits in 1963 having been condemned on 29th December 1962. A resident of Ferryhill since October 1945, the engine was cut up at Cowlairs on 27th September 1963! Its tender was salvaged for conversion to a heavyweight independent snowplough at Cowlairs. *I.W. Coulson (ARPT).*

One of the less fortunate A4s associated with Ferryhill: No.60005 SIR CHARLES NEWTON reveals that it was not coupled to a corridor tender in 1964. The locomotive has been cannibalised – some would say savaged – to keep the others in traffic. However, those nameplates were simply flame cut off the casing! The date of this image is 16th May 1964 and the A4 is dumped at the south-east corner of the shed near the turntable like some medieval corpse positioned where other A4s could see the treatment meted out to those who fail! The tender – No.5641 – was sold for scrap with the engine so it is perhaps a good time to remark on its history at this point. No.5641 was built in 1937 as part of a batch of ten replacement streamlined but non-corridor type tenders to be coupled to ten A3s which had given up their own corridor tenders for use with new A4s. Coupled initially to A3 No.60043 (2508) BROWN JACK, which had given up tender No.5330 to A4 No.60028 (4487) SEA EAGLE, No.5641 was only with the A3 from 2nd April 1937 to 19th April 1938 when it was uncoupled and got ready for coupling to our subject engine from 14th May 1938 until it was sold and cut up in 1964. Note that someone has rubbed away the paint on two areas of the locomotive; the casing near the dome cover, and on the streamlining on the tender top near the cab. The result looks like bare metal or even silver grey livery. No.60005 however was never in that early livery and came out in Garter blue in 1938. *John Boyes (ARPT).*

KEITH

Keith in the County of Banffshire was blessed with two engine sheds up to Nationalisation: One to the west of the station and belonging to the London Midland & Scottish Railway had origins going back to the Inverness & Aberdeen Junction Railway and was opened in August 1858. That shed was built with four covered roads but a two road section of the building on its north side was taken down and removed in 1868; apparently most of the salvaged stone was used in the building of Blair Atholl engine shed, a typical Highland Railway trait when money was tight! So for 80-years the two-road shed served the Highland, and latterly the LMS. BR however regarded the building and its facilities as surplus and effectively closed the depot in favour of the other shed at Keith which was located east of the station. This is the other shed on 26th May 1949. Built by the GNofSR and opened for business in 1856 this substantial stone-built structure would celebrate its centenary although somewhat modified from its appearance here. Photographed on a Thursday morning during an enthusiasts visit, the shed presented a typical mixture of former GNofSR motive power consisting 4-4-0s of various vintages and classes, whilst on the right is one of the twenty-five former Great Eastern Area B12 4-6-0s which were introduced to the Northern Scottish Area from April 1931. Identifiable are two un-named D40s – No.62262 and 'recently' ex-works (October 1948) No.62267 – both locally based. *K.H.Cockerill (ARPT).*

(*above*) **On 26th May 1949, No.62267 comes up the yard to show its fine pre-Grouping lines in early BR lined black.** (*below*) **On the same morning sister No.62247 shows off the earlier and more austere version of BR livery.** *Both K.H.Cockerill (ARPT).*

With an unidentified C16 tank engine for company, D40 No.62275 SIR DAVID STEWART rests inside Keith shed on Saturday 28th May 1955. This was one of the 1920-built batch which came out superheated and were some two tons heavier than the 1899 designed batches. Note the classification and allocation legends – courtesy of Inverurie – neatly painted on the bufferbeam; it's a shame the cleaning has become a secondary consideration. Modellers: Although only an internal detail, the modifications carried out to the top of the wall during the 1953 re-roofing are plain to see with brick, concrete and steel carefully blended. Those thick, stone built walls supporting everything date from 1856. Lighting at this time is a mixture of gas and newly installed electric. They'd never had it so good! *F.W.Hampson (ARPT)*.

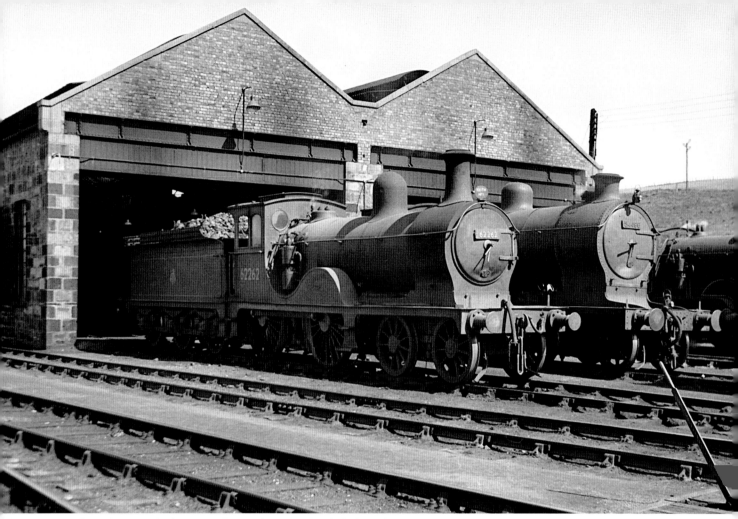

It must have been a glorious May in northern Scotland during 1955 as this image recorded on the 28th of the month testifies. The shed shows off its rebuilt face with the brick gables supported by steel lintels with wooden skirts to provide some wind and rain shelter from the westerlies' at least. Evidence of the actual raising of the roof can be seen on the side walls where new stonework and mortar courses were combined. Stabled outside the shed on this perfect afternoon are D40 No.62262 and visiting ex-Caley 3P No.54496 from Inverness. The D40 carries the KEITH No.1 target on its smokebox lamp-iron whilst the bufferbeam shows the classification and allocation of the 4-4-0. *F.W.Hampson (ARPT)*.

(*opposite page*) **D41s Nos.62242 and 62243 outside the shed on 5th October 1950!** This image affords us a reasonable view of the original gable end. No.62242 wears the correct 61C Keith shedplate whilst its bufferbeam still presents the shortened version of its previous and penultimate home at Kittybrewster which it left on 4th December 1949. The chances are that the K.BREWSTER legend remained until the withdrawal of 62242 in February 1953 but a visit to Inverurie for a light repair just a month after this image was recorded may well have seen it eradicated. Except for a five-year stint allocated to Kittybrewster during WW2, neighbour 62243 appears to have spent much of its life working from Keith but that was coming to an end because in the coming January the 4-4-0 was condemned! *K.H.Cockerill (ARPT)*.

This image of Keith engine shed pre-rebuilding could have been taken anytime from March 1943 to May 1946. It is included to show two things: what the shed building looked like at the end of the LNER era and the diversity of motive power to be found at the depot long before BR came into being. The ex-North Eastern G5, No.1914 had arrived at Keith in March 1943 at the culmination of an eventful life whereby it managed to work at the most southerly and northerly points of the LNER system. To sum up its lifetime allocation history might be the best illustration of its travels thus: Starting at Whitby, it went to Tyne Dock in February 1934; to Sunderland in February 1940; Borough Gardens September 1940; Stratford January 1941; Dunfermline October 1941; Parkhead January 1942; Kittybrewster November 1942; Keith March 1943. It was condemned 12th August 1952 and may well have been replaced by the ex-Caley 0-4-4T illustrated later? D41 No.6902 was another Keith resident – since March 1938 – and was to be renumbered 2246 on 1st September 1946. It too ended its days at Keith being condemned on 22nd August 1951. Although not discernible here, the D41 became to only one of its class to carry the longer smokebox during BR days. *C.J.B.Sanderson (ARPT)*.

(*above*) **Ex-LMS 2P No.40600 awaits attention on 8th June 1957. The 4-4-0 was a relative newcomer to 61C having left the Sou-Western' system in October 1952 for Dundee, then Kittybrewster in April 1954.** *F.W.Hampson (ARPT).* (*below*) **J36 No.65304 (ex-61A to 61C 25/3/57–19/6/61 to 61B), with a real custom-made tender cab, stables on the shed yard in 1957 with resident 3F 0-6-0T No.56348 (ex-61B to 61C 3/58–5/60 withdrawn) and an unidentified visiting Stanier Cl.5 for company.** *A.R.Thompson (ARPT).*

Keith on Saturday 16th May 1959 with another party of enthusiasts realising that the long hike to the north was worth every moment. Although by now the motive power on view did not contain any of the former erstwhile Great North classes, there were plenty of vintage pieces to see. Note that K2 No.61755 also has classification and shed name on the bufferbeam; this time Cowlairs were responsible. A visitor from Forres is ex-Caledonian 3P 4-4-0 No.54472 standing on No.4 road; this particular engine had spent most of its life working in the so-called 'Central Belt' of Scotland but had enjoyed a stint in the Highlands since late LMS days. It was soon to return south and this visit to Keith may well have been its last before transferring to St Rollox, Corkerhill and oblivion! This view of the shed building reveals the 1953 rebuilding and re-roofing with brick work topping off the gables. Steam was banished from the shed and indeed the area from 1961 as diesel locomotives and multiple units took over. The K2 was another steam locomotive which was enjoying its last summer of working; transferred to Keith on 4th March 1957 from Kittybrewster, condemnation would take place on 18th November 1959. Arriving at Eastfield shed on 11th February 1951, the 2-6-0 had spent its pre-Grouping life and LNER years working from sheds south of Selby. Ironically the Glasgow built locomotive ended its days at a scrapyard in Wishaw just a few miles from its birthplace. *N.W.Skinner (ARPT)*.

Ex-Caley 2P No.55185 arrived at Keith from Forfar in October 1952 followed by sister No.55221 from Beattock of all places, in September 1953. Photographed 16th May 1955, the tank is fitted with one of those austere chimneys which did little to enhance their looks. The reduction in the fleet of former GNofSR 4-4-0s brought these once rare – in Banffshire – classes of locomotive to Keith for the final years of steam motive power. Ideal for the branch workings entrusted to Keith these 0-4-4T enjoyed a final decade working some of the easiest jobs on BR. No.55185 remained at Keith to the end and was condemned in July 1961 to be taken on the short journey to Inverurie for breaking up. No.55221 managed to escape to Corkerhill but did little or no work there and was withdrawn in September 1961. *N.W.Skinner (ARPT).*

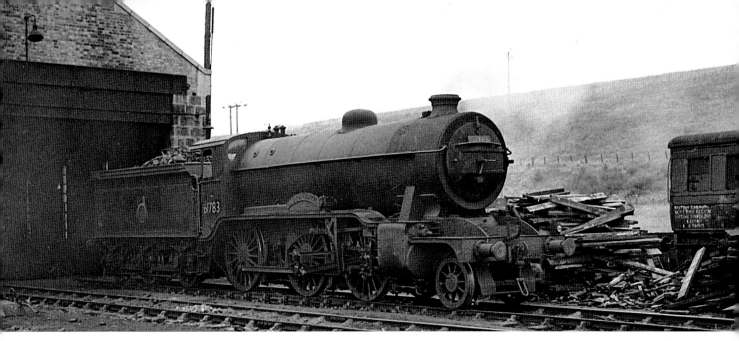

(*above*) **K2 No.61783 LOCH SHEIL** stables outside the shed on a less than ideal day in 1958. A latecomer to 61C, the 2-6-0 arrived at the beginning of September 1956 for what proved to be its final posting. Transferred to Scotland in July 1925 at Eastfield, this K2 managed to work at what were probably the most westerly (Fort William) and easterly (Kittybrewster) depots in Scotland – remember, your saw these facts here first! (*below*) **J72 No.68700** spent its formative years at Tyne Dock shed but in March 1932 with little work to keep it going in the depressed North-East, it was transferred to Keith. Three weeks later on 5th April it was sent to Kittybrewster where it remained until 14th January 1956 when it returned to 61C to end its days; after transfer to Scotland Inverurie became responsible for its maintenance. They also condemned it on 2nd December 1958 but afterwards sent it to Kilmarnock for breaking up where in March 1959 the deed was carried out! *Both A.R.Thompson (ARPT).*

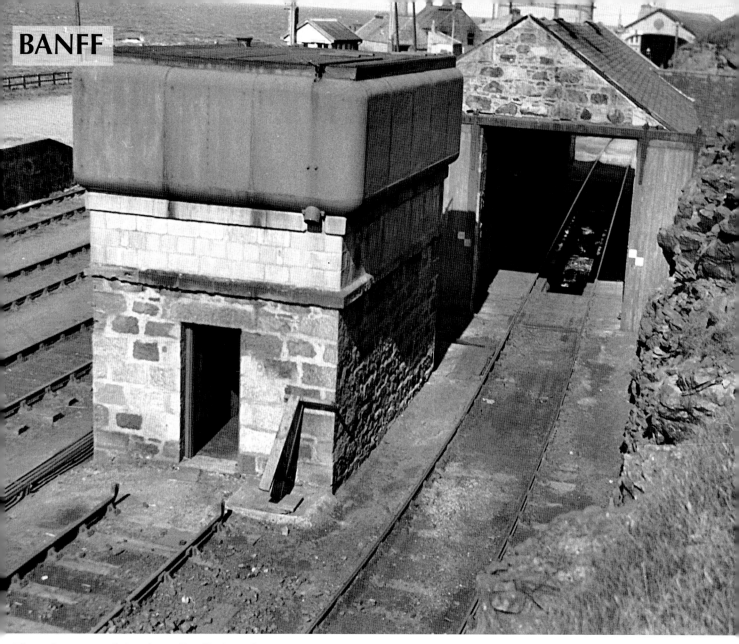

The rather cramped situation at Banff where they managed to build not only an engine shed but its associated water tank too. Alas no ground was available for a locomotive turntable but everything else was available; coaling, it appears, was carried out from a wagon located on the left-hand road whilst engines stood on the shed road. The shed was opened for business in July 1859 to shelter the motive power of the Banff, Portroy & Strathisla Railway but the GNofSR took over the branch workings in 1863 and then absorbed the railway in 1867. This shed lasted in use until July 1964 when the branch serving the nearby station closed; afterwards the engine shed was demolished. Note the upwards extension to the water tank base; now when was that built? *F.W.Hampson (ARPT).*

65

D40 No.62268 up-close outside the shed on 21st August 1955. The vantage point used to record the following image is seen above the shed with the gable ends of the Campbell Street residential properties peering over. Note the ubiquitous push-bike leaning against the grounded van body. Sometime before Grouping a small turntable was located on the shed road roughly where the 2P's bogie is situated. The single track leading off the table at right-angles southwards towards the high ground and then a building into which the track apparently entered. What the building was and when it was demolished is unknown so once again we ask our readers 'in the know' to contact the Publisher via the usual channels with chapter and verse of an explanation – thanks in anticipation! Suddenly the engine shed and its environs are looking interesting. *C.J.B.Sanderson (ARPT)*.

To many people this is a dream image of a location which can give so much information; this compiler is amongst that throng. Before we go any further, similar images exist of the station area too but alas they do not come under the remit for this album. In the meantime let us look at what is available especially for the modellers out there. The date is sometime during April 1955 and coming in from the sea like an invader, you would have to avoid the outcrops of rock which are thankfully exposed; once ashore you have the promenade railings to climb and then public seating forms to avoid. The road which leads to the station on the right of this image would have to be crossed to reach the signal box and the few sidings on the north side of the main line; note the signal box roof which has a mixture of sea salt, soot, bird droppings, and what looks like a faded painted name?! The two vans against the buffer stops are full of what might be termed 'official' graffiti with confusing numbers and unheard-of place names whilst a new-ish 16-ton mineral wagon awaits the coalman's attention. The private owner wagon – R.J.&M.CARR it seems – has appeared from another age and has got the attention of the coalman whose tipper truck is alongside and appearing somewhat puny compared to the rolling stock. Crossing the main line we have 2P No.62268 unmanned and quietly simmering away whilst the Westinghouse pump trips in every now and then to keep the brake pressure topped-up. Keith shed has supplied the D40 which is now in its final year of existence having used up all of its shopping trips some seventeen months previously. BR Standard tanks are waiting in the wings to take over these meagre branch workings before they are finally abolished altogether and a way of life is lost forever. Behind the 4-4-0 are two more 16-ton mineral wagons, full of what looks like (some good stuff in there) the depot's allocation of coal for the next month or so. And so to the engine shed: the open ground leading to the rising ground is hiding a secret and although revealing the sleeper-walled ash tip in this modern day, something existing decades beforehand is now missing. Beyond the wall is the allotment which was tended too by either the signalman or shed staff or both; the rich picking would provide a couple of families with plenty of vegetables and salad for much of the year. Next on the left we have the outbuildings attached to the shed at right-angles which probably contained stores, mess room, and perhaps an office. Finally, note the doors at this end of the shed which are hinged and shaped for the arched opening. The western end of the shed had sliding doors protecting a rectangular opening, a very unusual occurrence. So, what's holding you back from modelling such an idyllic location set right beside the seaside? *C.J.B.Sanderson (ARPT)*.

Sporting the target ELGIN No.1, D40 No.62264 comes onto Elgin shed yard during the afternoon of 28th May 1955. Looking rather smart for the period, the 4-4-0 had not been near works since January 1954 so the cleanliness was probably down to the staff at Elgin shed. Of course No.62264 was still allocated to Keith as it had been since March 1938 but the sub-shedding at Elgin appears to have done it no harm at all. The engine and tender ended up in this livery after a General overhaul in December 1953; before that No.62264 had hauled around a tender with the BRITISH RAILWAYS legends simply painted out for nearly three years from February 1951. *F.W.Hampson (ARPT).*

D40 No.62269 reveals another angle of this handsome class to the lens on 28th May 1955. An enthusiast with camera negotiates the transition from cab to steps as the former appears somewhat crowded. The Keith based engine is turned ready to work home and the tender cab fixture is ready to be removed; these temporary fixtures were used on those engines working the branch lines where turning was impossible. This image shows to best effect the original Westinghouse brake and its simple but efficient method of applying the shoes to the coupled wheels. Vacuum ejectors were fitted to three of the five Neilson-built saturated members of this class in June 1908 to enable them to work Highland stock between Aberdeen and Inverness but our subject here was not so fitted until March 1934. However, by then B12 had taken over much of the main-line workings and the D40s were used on branch services. Note the rather neat arrangement of handrails on both locomotive cab and tender. The Route Availability of 4 meant these engines could work virtually everywhere on the Great North system. Inverurie-built (their No.6 of July 1913) No.62269 was condemned at the end of the summer timetable and afterwards taken to the former G&SWR locomotive works at Kilmarnock where it was broken up. *F.W.Hampson (ARPT).*

No.62269 from the front in May 1955; the image reveals the steam heating connection, necessary for branch work, along with the dual-brake hoses. The lamp iron on the cab sidesheet was fitted to all the saturated engines but none of the superheated members of D40 were so fitted. *F.W.Hampson (ARPT)*.

BR Standard Cl.2 No.78053 looking rather smart alongside the water tower at Elgin on Saturday 22nd June 1957. Along with sister No.78054, this 2-6-0 started its operational life at Motherwell shed in November 1955 but eleven months later was transferred to Ferryhill shed in Aberdeen. After less than a month at 61B they were moved on to Keith where they settled in until June 1961 when all the steam locomotives in the old GNofSR area were ejected. The pair ended up from whence they came at 61B. When they arrived in this part of Scotland those enclosed cabs were totally appreciated by the enginemen and gave the engines more versatility than those with conventional open cabs in being able to travel tender first without fear of freezing the crew in extreme weather conditions. Both 78053 and 78054 had premature withdrawals going in July 1964 and December 1965 respectively. The substantial water tank base is supporting a hefty weight which alas is unknown in quantity but the tank itself has a plate on its side with the legend W. Kinnon & Co., Engineers, Aberdeen. *C.J.B.Sanderson (ARPT).*

1929 Derby-built 2P No.40622 stables outside Elgin shed on Monday 22nd August 1960 during its last full year of operation. Indeed the shed was itself was experiencing its last full year of steam occupation; it later became a dump to store unserviceable North British Locomotive Co. built D6100 Type 2 diesel-electric locomotives but after they were taken away for scrap, it stood until at least the end of the Millennium garaging council vehicles. No.40622 was one of the half-dozen members of her class which had gravitated to Keith in the previous four years as replacements for B12s, and K2s. The full listing of the Keith 2P 4-4-0s was No.40600 which with 40622 transferred to 61C from Kittybrewster in October 1956; followed by 40617 and 40618 from Hurlford in April 1957. When No.40617 was withdrawn in November 1959 Nos.40603 and 40604, also ex 61A, came to Keith as replacements. By July 1961 all the 4-4-0s had departed from 61C either through transfer or withdrawal and steam was replaced by diesel. The tender coupled to No.40622 – No.3953 – started life behind sister No.(40)604 in 1928 and was probably changed at Keith when the two locomotives were brought together by the November 1959 transfer, although the pair had been together at Kittybrewster for many a year so the change could easily have happened there, not to mention Inverurie works. Note that the BR emblem is one of the wrong-facing examples. These 2Ps had all started life at various sheds on the former Glasgow & South Western section of the LMS in the late 1920s and this final posting to the GNofSR section was to be their first and last transfer from south-west Scotland. Elgin engine shed dated from about the same time as Kittybrewster whose design it followed very closely. *C.J.B.Sanderson (ARPT).*